Horace Walpole

Notes on the Poems of Alexander Pope

Horace Walpole

Notes on the Poems of Alexander Pope

ISBN/EAN: 9783743345836

Manufactured in Europe, USA, Canada, Australia, Japa

Cover: Foto ©ninafisch / pixelio.de

Manufactured and distributed by brebook publishing software
(www.brebook.com)

Horace Walpole

Notes on the Poems of Alexander Pope

Horace Walpole's Notes to Pope.

MESSIAH.
V. 71.

On rifted rocks, the dragon's late abodes.]

THIS line is an exact picture of, & probably taken from, Wharncliff in Yorkshire, the fabled Den of the Dragon of Wantley. It belongs to Wortley Montagu, & was possibly visited by Pope during his intimacy with Lady Mary Wortley.

B

The Dying Chriſtian to his Soul.

O D E.

V. 1.

Vital ſpark of heav'nly flame !]

Imitated from theſe Lines of Flatman

When on my ſick bed I languiſh,
Full of sorrow, full of anguiſh,
Fainting, gaſping, trembling, crying,
Panting, groaning, ſpeechleſs, dying—
Methinks I hear ſome gentle spirit ſay,
Be not fearfull, come away !

See the Adventurer No. 63.

AN
ESSAY
ON
CRITICISM.
V. 460.

Pride, Malice, Folly, against Dryden rose,
In various shapes of Parsons, Critics, Beaus;]

L'ignorance & l'erreur à ses naissantes pieces,
En habits de Marquis, en robes de Comtesses
Venoient pour diffamer son chef-d'œuvre
nouveau.
BOILEAU. See Advent. No. 63.

V. 608.

Still run on Poets, in a raging vein,
Ev'n to the dregs and squeezings of the brain,
Strain out the last dull droppings of their sense,
And rhyme with all the rage of Impotence.]

Me would you have, me yr faint passion
prove,
The dregs & droppings of enervate Love?
Nourmahal in Aurunzebe.

THE

RAPE of the *LOCK*.

CANTO II.

V. 29.

Th' advent'rous Baron the bright locks admir'd.]
Lord Petre.

CANTO IV.

She faid; then raging to Sir Plume repairs.]
Sir George Brown.

ELOISA

TO

ABELARD.

V. 48.

No happier tafk thefe faded eyes purfue ;
To read and weep is all they now can do.]
Thefe eyes,
Where now without a boaft some luftre lies,
No longer fhall their little honours keep,
Shall only be of ufe to read and weep.
PRIOR's *Celia to Damon.*

V. 170.

And breathe a browner horror on the woods.]
And breathe a browner horror on the plain.
DRYDEN'S Fables.

ELEGY

to the MEMORY of an

UNFORTUNATE LADY.

The name of this Lady was *Withinbury,*
pronounced *Winbury :* the seat of her family
was *Chiras Court,* vulgarly *Cheyney's Court,*
situated under Frome Hill & forming
nearly a triangle with *Home Lacey* &
Hampton Lacey. It is said that she did not
stab, but hang herself.

*What beck'ning ghost, along the moonlight shade
Invites my step, and points to yonder glade ;*]

What gentle ghoſt beſprent with april dew,
Hayls me ſo solemnly to yonder yew?
And beck'ning woes me, &c.

> BEN· JONSON'S *Elegy on the Marchioneſs of Wincheſter. See* WARTON'S *Notes on Spenser, Vol.* 2. *p.* 12.

PROLOGUE

TO

M^r. *ADDISON'S Tragedy.*

OF

CATO.

V. 23.

While CATO *gives his little Senate laws.*]
Borrowed by himſelf in his satire on
Addiſon :—

Like Cato give his little Senate laws.

To the Author of the Essay on Man.
C., probably Lord Cornbury.

To the Author of the Essay on Man.
R. D., probably Rob. Dodsley.

AN

ESSAY ON MAN:
being the first book of
ETHIC EPISTLES
TO

HENRY ST. JOHN,
L. BOLINGBROKE.

EPISTLE XI.

V. 11.

Alike in ignorance, his reason such,
Whether he thinks too little, or too much;]

What a Chimera then is man! what a
confused Chaos! what a subject of contra-

diction; a profeſsed judge of all things, and
yet a feeble worm of the earth! the great
depoſitary and guardian of truth, and yet a
mere huddle of uncertainty! the glory and
the ſcandal of the Univerſe.

PASCAL i. *Adv. No.* 63.

V. 31.

Superior Beings, when of late they ſaw
A mortal man unfold all Nature's law,
Admir'd ſuch wiſdom in an earthly ſhape,
And ſhew'd a NEWTON *as we ſhew an Ape.*]

Utque movet nobis imitatrix ſimia viſum,
Sic nos cœlicolis, quoties cervice ſuperbâ
Ventoſi gradimur—
Simia cœlicolûm riſuſḉ; jocuſque deorum eſt
Tunc homo, quum temerè ingenio confidit
    & audet
Abdita naturæ ſcrutari arcanaque Divûm.

PALINGENIUS *see Advent. No.* 63.

or this Thought might have been taken
from Heraclitus, who said, The wiſeſt of

men compared with a God, will appear an ape in wifdom & beauty & every other Excellence.

See Sydenham's *tranfl. of* Plato's
Hippias, p. 61.

EPISTLE III.

V. 45.

While man exclaims "fee all things for my ufe!"
" See man for mine," replies a pamper'd goofe;]

Man fcruples not to fay that he enjoyeth the Heavens & the Elements, as if all had been made & ftill move only for him. In this fenfe a Gofling may fay as much & perhaps with more fenfe & juftice.

Charron. *See Advent. No.* 63.

EPISTLE IV.

V. 117.

As that the virtuous Son is ill at eafe,
When his lewd father gave the dire difeafe,]

When his lewd fire tranfmitted the difeafe.

c

V. 125.

When the loose Mountain tumbles from on high
Shall Gravitation cease as you go by?]

If a good man be passing by an infirm building, just in the article of falling; can it be expected that God should suspend the force of gravitation till he is gone by, in order to his deliverance?

WOLLASTON.   *See Adv. No.* 63.

V. 369.

Form'd by thy converse, happily to steer
From grave to gay, from lively to severe.]

*   *   *   d'une voix legere
Passer du grave au doux, du plaisant au severe.

BOILEAU.

EPISTLES.

TO

SEVERAL PERSONS.

EPISTLE I. TO SIR RICHARD TEMPLE, LORD VISCOUNT COBHAM.

V. 67.

Who combats bravely, is not therefore brave ;
He dreads a Death-bed like the meaneſt ſlave.]

This alludes to Mon^{sr}. Auverquerque a Dutch General in Qu· Anne's wars. Having a painfull chronical diſorder he was always trying to get killed ; one day having led the D. of Marlb. too near to the Enemy, to ſhow him a new battery, one of the Duke's aid-de-camp's advertiſed his Grace of the danger : he took no notice ; being again admoniſhed, he replied peeviſhly, Why do you tell me of it? don't you ſee that old Fool there?" This Story was probably told to Pope by Lord Cobham, to whom this Epiftle is addrefsed, and who one day related it as an Inftance of the D. of Marlborough's refolution, when the Duke of Argyle had been queftioning that Great Man's courage.

V. 121.

While One *there is who charms us with his fpleen.*]

L^d. Cobham.

V. 140.

Who would not praife Patritio's *high defert.*]

L^d. Godolphin The Treafurer.

V. 146.

Triumphant Leaders, at an Army's head,
Hemm'd round with glories, pilfer cloth or bread,
As meanly plunder, as they bravely fought,
Now fave a People, and now fave a Groat.]

Duke of Marlborough.

V. 150.

What made   *   *   *
A perjur'd Prince a Leaden Saint *revere?*
A god-lefs Regent tremble at a Star?]
Philip Duke of Orleans.

V. 154.

The Throne a Bigot *keep.*]
Philip 5th.

V. 154.

A Genius *quit,*]
the Regent.

V. 156.

Europe, a Woman,]
Czarina Elizabeth.

V. 156.
Child,]

Louis 15th.

V. 156.
or Dotard rule ;]
Benedict 13ᵗʰ.

V. 180.
Clodio the Scorn and Wonder of our days.]
Duke of Wharton.

V. 228.

Behold a rev'rend Sire, whom Want of grace
Has made the father of a nameless race.]
Blackburne Archbiſhop of York.

V. 233.
A Salmon's belly, Helluo, was thy fate :
The Doctor call'd, declares all help too late.
Mercy ! cries Helluo, mercy on my ſoul !
Is there no hope ? alas ! then bring the Jowl.]

— puiſque il faut que je meure,
Sans faire tant de façon,
Qu'on m'apporte tout à l'heure
Le reſte de mon poiſſon.

FONTAINE. *See Adv. No.* 63.

EPISTLE II. TO A LADY.

M^{rs}. Blount. Warburton having quarreld with her, pretended this Epiſtle was addreſs'd to an imaginary Perſon.

V. 7.

Arcadia's *Counteſs, here in ermin'd pride,*]

Mary Howe, 3^d. Wife of Thomas Earl of Pembroke.

V. 24.

As Sapho's *diamonds with her dirty ſmock ;*]

L^y Mary Wortley.

V. 45.

'Twas thus Calypſo *once our hearts alarm'd,*]

Ann Griffin Daughter of Lady Mohun, wife of William Earl of Harrington.

V. 53.

Narcissa's *nature tolerably mild,*]

Elizabeth Gerard, 2^d Wife of James Duke of Hamilton.

V. 69.

Flavia's *a Wit, has too much ſenſe to* pray,]

Henrietta Dſs. of Marlborough, wife of Lord Godolphin.

V. 89.

Or her who laughs at Hell, but (like her Grace)
Cries oh ! how charming if there's no ſuch
place !]

Flavia above.

V. 155.

While what fatigues the Ring.]

In Hyde Park.

In the additional Characters, publifhed in Bifhop Warburton's Edition, Atofsa is known to be Sarah Dfs. of Marlborough. Cloe, I fufpect, from fome touches & from its preceding the queen's character, to be meant for Lady Suffolk, the King's Miftrefs, and to have been kept back, becaufe Pope was intimate with her. There is a paffage that feems taken from Lee's Duke of Guife, She while a Lover, &c. The Duke fays, his miftrefs was fo cold, that when his breeches were down, fhe afked him what the ftuff coft a yard.

EPISTLE III.

TO THE RIGHT HONOURABLE ALLEN

LORD BATHURST.

V. 44.

Sir, Spain has fent a thoufand jars of oyl:]
The rich Arabian fills his ample vafe
With facred incenfe; Ethiopia fends

D

A thoufand courfers fleeter than the wind,
And their black riders darken all the
    plains, &c.

              Young's *Busiris.*

V. 50.

And Worldly *crying coals from ftreet to
    ftreet,*]

Wortley Montagu.

V. 107.

But rev'rend S—— with a fofter air,]

S^r. Rob. Sutton.

V. 111.

*Damn'd to the Mines, an equal fate betides,
The Slave that digs it, and the Slave that hides.*]

    This thought, falfe wit as it is, was bor-
row'd from a book called *the caufes of the
decay of Chriftian piety,* where the pun is
helped out by a piece of Latin. It has

always been held the fevereft treatment of slaves and malefactors, damnare ad metalla, to force them to dig in the mines : now this is the covetous man's lot, from which he is never to expect a releafe.

See Adv. No. 63.

V. 129.

The Crown of Poland, venal twice an age,
To juft three millions ftinted modeft Gage.]

Monfieur de Gage, a Spanifh General, Brother to L^d. Vifcount Gage.

V. 131.

But nobler fcenes MARIA's *dreams unfold,*
Hereditary Realms, and worlds of gold,
Congenial fouls ! whofe life one Av'rice joins,
And one fate buries in th' Afturian mines.]

Lady Mary Herbert, fifter of the laft Marquis of Powis, had made a prodigious fortune in the Miffiffipi, & refufed the Duke of Bouillon, being determined to marry nobody but a Sovereign Prince; but refuſing to realiſe, loſt the whole, & met Gage in the Aſturian mines. Some years after, the young Pretender being at Madrid, ſhe ſent to deſire to ſee him. He found her in a garret, ſo poor that ſhe could not riſe for want of clothes; he gave her his greatcoat, & what money he had about him. In 1766, when I was at Paris ſhe and Gage were both alive at Paris; he died in May that year. She was in a lodging given to her by the Prince of Conti at the Temple, & in April of the ſame year recovered two annuities & the arrears from the Earl of Powis, by a ſentence of the House of Lords.

EPISTLE IV.

TO RICHARD EARL OF BURLINGTON.

V. 19.

See ſportive fate, to puniſh aukward pride,
Bids BUBO *build, and ſends him ſuch a Guide.*]

Mr. Doddington.

V. 75.

Or cut wide views thro' Mountains to the Plains.]

At Moor Park by Mr. Styles.

EPISTLE VII.

TO Mr. ADDISON.

Poor Vadius long with learned spleen devour'd,
Can taste no pleasure since his Shield was
scour'd;

Dr. Woodward. His housemaid scoured his famous antique shield.

EPISTLE VIII.

TO Mr. JERVAS.

V. 45.

Thence Beauty, waking all her forms, supplies
An Angel's sweetness, or Bridgwater's eyes.]

Eliz. Countess of Bridgwater, 3d Daughter of 1. D. of Marlbro.

V. 60.

And other Beauties envy Wortley's eyes ;]
Frances, D^r. of L^d. Weymouth, and wife
of S^r. Robert Wortley: mother of Lady
Carteret.

V. 75.

With Zeuxis' Helen thy Bridgewater vie,]
Lady Newbury.

V. 76.

And these be sung till Granville's Myra die ;]
Jervas was in love with Lady Bridgwater.

EPISTLE XI.

TO D^r. ARBUTHNOT.

V. 25.

Poor Cornus sees his frantick wife elope,
And curses Wit and Poetry and Pope.]
R. L^d. Walpole.

V. 139.

The courtly Talbot,]
Duke of Shrewſbury.

V. 149.

Like gentle Fanny's.]
Ld. Hervey.

V. 232.

Sate full-blown Bufo, *puff'd by ev'ry quill ;*]
Earl of Halifax.

V. 280.

The firſt Lampoon Sir Will.]
Sir W. Yonge.

V. 280.

or Bubo *makes.*]
Doddington.

V. 305.

Let SPORUS *tremble*—]

Lᵈ. Hervey.

V. 341.

But ſtoop'd to Truth, and moraliz'd his song;]

Fierce wars & faithfull loves ſhall moralize my ſong.

SPENCER, *Introd. to Fairy Queen.*

V. 380.

Let the two CURLS *of Town and Court, abuſe*]

Lord Hervey.

V. 393.

Nor marrying Diſcord in a noble wife,]

This line perhaps had two alluſions. It might allude to Dryden, who married a ſiſter of the Earl of Berkſhire, whom he did not love, probably from her over fondneſs, as appeared by a ſtory related of him. One day coming into his library, Lady Eliz. Dryden fd to him, " Mr. Dryden, you are always poring upon books—I wiſh I was a book." " Then" replied the Poet with an oath, " I wiſh you were an almanack that I might change you every year." Mr Pope too by ſaying he did not marry a noble wife, might hint at being married to Mrs Blount, as it is believed he was. Dr Young whom Pope did not love, was alſo married to a noble wife, a ſiſter of the Earl of Litchfield, but as I do not know that they diſagreed, Pope might not refer to theſe too; but he might alſo mean Mr Addiſon who was made ſo unhappy by his wife the Counteſs Dowager of Warwick, that it was ſuppoſed to make him take to drinking.

EPITAPHS.

I.

On

CHARLES *Earl of* DORSET

in the Church of

Wythyham *in* Suſſex.

V. 5.

Yet ſoft his Nature tho' ſevere his Lay.]
The beſt good man, with the worſt-
natur'd Muſe.

VIII.

On M^r. ELIJAH FENTON.
V. 2.

Here lies an honeſt Man :]
This plain Floor
Believe me, Reader, can ſay more,

Than many a braver Marble can ;
Here lies a truly honeſt man.

CRASHAW.

IX.

On Mʳ. GAY.

V. 1.

*Of Manners gentle, of Affeƈtions mild ;
In Wit, a Man ; Simplicity, a Child :*]

Imitated from Dryden on Mʳˢ. Killigrew,

Her wit was more than man,
Her innocence a child.

X.

Intended for Sir IsAAC NEWTON *in*
Weſtminſter-Abbey.

Nature and Nature's Laws lay hid in night :
GOD *ſaid,* Let Newton be! *and all was light.*]

Naturæ facies caligine merſa jacebat ;
Tandem Newtonus *ſe* oſtendit et omnia Secum.*

TH. ASHTON.

CLOE:

A CHARACTER.

She while a Lover pants upon her breaſt,
Can mark the figures on an Indian Cheſt :]

Once, when my breeches were down, ſhe
aſked me what the ſtuff coſt a yard.

DRYDEN's *Duke of Guiſe.*

---

* Ovid.

THE
FIRST SATIRE
of the second BOOK of
HORACE.

POPE & FORTESCUE.

V. 3.

Scarce to wife Peter complaifant enough,]
P. Walter.

V. 6.

Lord Fanny fpins a thoufand fuch a day.]
Lᵈ· Hervey.

V. 23.

What ? like Sir Richard rumbling, rough, and
fierce.]
Blackmore.

V. 46.

Darty his Ham-pye ;]
Mr. Dartiguenave.

V. 81.

Slander or Poison dread from Delia's rage.]
Lady Deloraine.

V. 82.

Hard words or hanging if your Judge be ∗]
Page.

V. 83.

From furious Sappho scarce a milder fate,]
Lady Mary Wortley.

V. 107.

Dash the proud Gamester in his gilded Car :]
Capt. Jansen.

V. 123.

Know all the diftant din that world can keep,
Rolls o'er my Grotto, and but fooths my fleep.]

Mr Pope's garden at Twickenham was
feparated by the Road but connected by a
Grotto dug under it.

THE

SECOND SATIRE

OF THE

SECOND BOOK

OF

HORACE.

V. 49.

Avidien or his Wife.]

M^r. Wortley & Lady Mary.

V. 181.

Shades that to BACON *could retreat afford.*]

Gourhambury near St Albans.

V. 182.

Become the portion of a booby Lord ;]

Ld Grimſton.

V. 183.

And Hemſley, once proud Buckingham's delight,
Slides to a Scriv'ner or a city Knight.]

Sir Charles Duncomb.

THE
FIRST EPISTLE
OF THE
FIRST BOOK
OF
HORACE.

V. 85.

BARNARD *in spirit, sense, and truth abounds.*]
Sr John.

V. 88.

As Bug now has,]
Duke of Kent.

V. 88.

And Dorimant would have.]
Doddington.

F

V. 112.

If honeſt S ∗ z take ſcandal at a ſpark,]
Schutz.

V. 131.

Some win rich Widows by their Chine and Brawn :]
Mr Nugent.

V. 150.

The Fool whoſe Wife elopes ſome thrice a quarter,]
Lord Vane.

THE
SIXTH EPISTLE.
OF THE
FIRST BOOK
OF
HORACE.

V. 42.

Sigh while his Cloë blind to Wit and Worth
Weds the rich Dulnefs of fome Son of earth?]

Mifs Foley.

V. 57.

And defp'rate Mifery lays hold on Dover.]

A Phyfician who prefcribed quickfilver.

V. 116.

So Ruffel did, but could not eat at night.]

Ld Edward Ruffel.

V. 122.

K——l's lewd Cargo, or Ty——y's Crew,]

Kinnoul.   Tyrawley.

THE

FIRST EPISTLE

OF THE

SECOND BOOK

OF

HORACE.

V. 22.

Thofe Suns of Glory pleafe not till they fet.]

Thofe Suns of glory rife not till they fet.

WALLER.

V. 105.

Or damn all Shakespear, like th' affected Fool
At court, who hates whate'er he read at school.]

Ld Hervey.

V. 176.

Nor ——'s self e'er tells more fibs than I.]

Hervey.

V. 215.

And in our own (excuse some Courtly stains)
No whiter page than Addison remains.]

Addison wrote an epistle to Q. Caroline
when Princess.

V. 289.

How Van wants grace, who never wanted Wit!]

Vanbrugh.

V. 293.

To make poor Pinky eat with vast applause!]

Penkethman.

THE

SECOND EPISTLE

OF THE

SECOND BOOK

OF

HORACE.

V. 24.

I think Sir Godfry ſhould decide the ſuit ;]
Kneller.

V. 139.

*Lord! how we ſtrut thro' Merlin's Cave, to ſee
No Poets there but Stephen, you, and me.*]
Duck.

V. 234.

All Worldly's hens, nay partridge, ſold to town.]
Wortley Montagu.

THE

FIRST ODE

OF THE

FOURTH BOOK

OF

HORACE.

V. 10.

*There spread round M * * y all your blooming
   Loves.*]

Murray.

THE

SECOND SATIRE

OF THE

FIRST BOOK

OF

HORACE.

V. 16.

But not Sir H——t for he does the same.]
Sir Herbert Packington.

V. 18.

Fufidia thrives in Money, Land, and Stocks :]
Lady Mary Wortley.

V. 21.

She turns her very Sister to a job,]
Lady Marr.

V. 30.

Sweet Moll and Jack are Civet-Cat and Boar:]
Lᵈ & Lʸ Hervey.

V. 39.

My Lord of L——n chancing to remark.]
London.

V. 44.

Or others spouses like my Lord of ——.]
York.   Archbp. Blackburn.

V. 45.

May no such Praise (cries J——s) e'er be mine!]
Jefferies.

V. 46.

J——s who bows at H——sb——w's hoary
  Shrine.]
Lady Hilsborow.

G

V. 62.

And yet some care of S——st should be had ;]
Salluft.   Suppofed to mean Ld Bolin-
broke.

V. 121.

To all defects T——y not so blind :]
Tyrawley.

V. 125.

A Lady's Face is all you see undress'd ;
(For none but Lady M— shows the rest.)]
Mary.

V. 133.

Not thus at N—dh—m's ;]
Needhams.

V. 158.

So B—t cries, Philosopher and Rake !]
Bathurft.

V. 177.

No Miſtreſs H—ysh—m near, no Lady B—ck:]

Heysham, Buck.   Lady Buck and M^rs.
Heysham were Friends of Lady Hilſ-
borough, but engaged in a plot with her
Huſband, who had long connived at her
Intrigue with M^r. Jefferies, to go a Party
of pleaſure to the Spa, where they caught
the Lady & her lover together, who was
forced to compound with the Huſband.

V. 179.

This truth let L—l, J—ys, O—w tell,]

Liddel, Jeffries, Onſlow.

THE

SATIRES

OF

Dʳ. JOHN DONNE,

DEAN OF ST. PAUL'S,

Verfified.

THE SECOND SATIRE OF Dʳ. JOHN DONNE.

V. 36.

Who live like S——tt——n,]

General Sutton.

V. 66.

If Peter deigns to help you to your own :]

Peter Walter.

V. 87.

Or when a Duke to Janſen punts at White's,]
Wrioth. Duke of Bedford.

THE FOURTH SATIRE OF Dr. JOHN DONNE.

V. 73.

But Ho * * y for a period of a mile.]
Bp. Hoadley.

V. 186.

Where Contemplation prunes her ruffled wings,]

Where with her beſt nurſe Contemplation
She plumes her feathers & lets grow her
      wings,
That in the various buſtles of reſort
Were all too ruffled.

           MILTON's *Comus.*

EPILOGUE

TO THE

S A T I R E S

IN TWO DIALOGUES.

DIALOGUE I.

V. 12.

Bubo obferves, he lafh'd no fort of Vice :]
Doddington.

V. 14.

H—ggins knew the Town.]
Higgins.

V. 17.

In rev'rend Su—n note fome fmall neglect.]
Sʳ Robᵗ. Sutton.

V. 39.

A joke on JEKYLL.]
Sʳ. Jofeph Jekyll, Mʳ. of the Rolls.

V. 68.

*   *   *   *the flow of Y—ng !*]

Sʳ W. Yonge.

V. 71.

That Firſt was H—vy's,]

Hervy.

V. 71.

*   *   *F—x's next, and then.*]

Steph. Fox, afterwards Lᵈ Ilcheſter, mov'd the Addreſs of Condolence on the Queen's Death. Lᵈ Hervey wrote a latin Epitaph on Her. He ſhew'd it to Dʳ Middleton & Dʳ Friend, the Maſter of Weſtminſter, who made ſome corrections in it,—but never to Dʳ Bland, Dean of Durham, with whom he was not acquainted.

V. 72.

The S—te's.]

Senate's.

V. 72.

And then H—y's once agen.]

Hervey's.

V. 92.

Immortal S——k,]

Ld Selkirk.

V. 92.

And grave De—re !]

L^d. Delawar.

V. 113.

Who ſtarves a Siſter or forſwears a Debt.]

This whole line alludes to Lady Mary
Wortley, whoſe ſiſter, Lady Mar being diſorder'd was ſhut up by Her & us'd barbar-
ouſly. The Debt was to a Monſ^r de Rure-
monde, a French man who had follow'd
her to London ; ſhe perſuaded him to let

her lay out above £2000 in the ſtocks for him; as ſoon as She had got it, ſhe told him her Huſband had diſcover'd their intrigue & would murder him if he did not fly; after which ſhe denied the Debt; he threaten'd to ſend her letters to her Huſband, on which ſhe tried to get Lᵈ Mar & Lᵈ Stair to fight him.

DIALOGUE II.

V. 1.

'Tis all a Libel—Paxton (Sir) will ſay.]

Sollicitor to the Treaſury.

V. 61.

As S——k if he lives will love the PRINCE.]

Ld Selkirk.

V. 71.

SECKER *is decent.*]

Bp. of Oxford.

V. 71.

RUNDEL *has a Heart,*]

Bp. of Derry.

V. 72.

Manners with candour are to BENSON *giv'n,*]

Bp. of Glocefter.

V. 73.

To BERKLEY, *ev'ry Virtue under Heav'n.*]

Dean of

V. 92.

And if yet higher the proud Lift fhould end,]

Frederic Pr. of Wales.

V. 108.

Each Mother aſks it for her booby ſon.]
Dſs of Buckingham.

V. 109.

Each Widow aſks it for the Beſt of Men.]
Mrs. Nugent.

V. 115.

Are they not rich? what more can they pretend?]
Alderman Barber offer'd him money to be mention'd with Encomium in his works, but was refus'd.

V. 130.

Spirit of ARNALL ! *aid me while I lye.*]
Author of the Free Briton.

V. 159.

Againſt your Worſhip then had S——k writ?]
Selkirk.

V. 160.

Or P—ge pour'd forth the Torrent of his Wit?]
Page.

V. 161.

Or grant the Bard whose diſtich all commend.]
M^r. Doddington.

V. 163.

To W——le guilty of ſome venial ſin ;]
Walpole.

V. 165.

The Prieſt whoſe Flattery bedropt the Crown,]
Dr. Gilbert, afterwards Archbiſhop of York, affected to cry in the pulpit, preaching on the death of the Queen.

V. 167.

And how did, pray, the florid Youth offend,]
Step. Fox.

V. 241.

And may descend from M———n to Stair,]

Ld Mordington kept a gaming house in Covent Garden.

V. 244.

Or beam good Digby ! *from a heart like thine,*]

Ld Digby.

THE DUNCIAD:

TO

D^r. JONATHAN SWIFT.

Book II.

V. 140.

And Tutchin *flagrant from the scourge, below.*]

There is a print of him with this motto, Pulcrum est pro Patriâ mori.

V. 73.

From ſhelves to ſhelves ſee greedy Vulcan *roll,*]

There had'ſt thou pleas'd either to dine or ſup,
Had made a meal for Vulcan to lick up.

Ben Jonson. *See* Warton's
Notes on Spenser, *v.* 2. *p.* 13.

WAGERS AT WHITE'S.

WAGERS AT WHITE'S.

L^d. Lincoln betts L^d. Winchilſea one hundred guineas to Fifty guineas that the Dutcheſs of Marlborough does not ſurvive the Dutcheſs of Cleveland. 1743.

Mr. Reynolds wagers Mr. Fanſhawe five guineas that the Eldeſt Son of Lord Seymour would not have the title of Lord during the life of his grandfather the preſent Duke of Somerſet, it being underſtood that the preſent Lord Seymour is neither a Marqueſs nor Earl. Sep^t. 18th. 1752.

L^d. Montfort wagers Sir J^n. Bland one hundred guineas that Mr. Naſh outlives Mr. Cibber. Novemb^r 4th. 1754.

I

58 *Wagers at White's.*

NOTE (*in another hand*).

Both L^d. M. & Sir J. B. put an end to their own lives before the Bet was decided.

L^d. Rochfort wagers Mr. Maxwell one hundred guineas, his N°. againſt M^r. Maxwell's in Hogarth's Raffle, if neither have the prize the Bett is void.   1755.

L^d. Duncannon is to pay Col. Waldegrave one Hundred guineas when the Engliſh are not in poſſeſſion of Gibraltar. June ye 2^d.   1756.

Lord Eglintoune betts Mr. Vernon two hundred guineas that he finds a man ſhall kill twenty ſnipes in three & twenty ſhotts, before the 20th of May.   Jan. 23^d.   1757.

Mr. Fanſhawe wagers Mr. Fanquier one guinea that if Mr. Harley comes to the Houſe of Commons the firſt day of ſitting He comes in a Red Gown.   1761.

L^d. March bets L^d. Orford that Sir Robert Rich L^d. Ligonier & Genl. Guife are not all Living on the 19th day of January 1765. July 15th. 1764.

A betts B that B has never been as far from London as C, nor never will be as far as long as He lives.

Quere is this a proper Bett or no?

Memorandum, C has been within a League of the Canaries.

Mr. Meynell is defired to give his opinion upon this Bett.

My opinion is that it is a proper Bett. W. Meynell. March ye 24. 1766.

Coll. Burgoyne betts M^r. Cox twenty guineas that the N°. 37463 has a better chance in the prefent Lottery than the N°. 54563, if neither is drawn prize, the laft drawn Ticket to win. Oct. 27th. 1768.

The D. of Queenfbury bets M^r. Grenville

10 gˢ. to 5. that Mʳ. Fox does not ſtand a poll for Weſtminſter if the Parlᵗ. ſhould be diſſolved within a month from the date hereof. N. B. if a *Coalition* takes place between Mʳ. Pitt & Mʳ. Fox this bet to be off.   March 3.   1784.

Mʳ. Brummell bets Mʳ. Oſborne twenty guineas that he (Mʳ. B.) is married before him (Mʳ. O.).   16ᵗʰ. March.   1798.

Col. Copley has given Mʳ. F. Colman ſeven ſhillings to receive fifty guineas whenever the preſent Lord Rivers marries. Sept. 5ᵗʰ.   1805.

Mʳ. Steward bets Mʳ. F. Delme five gui-neas that Lord Grenville and Mʳ. Fox are Divided & that Lord Grenville joins the late *Mʳ. Pitt's Party* within ſix months from this day, provided his preſent Majeſty is then living.   February 2ᵈ.   1806.

Lord de Clifford received ten ſhillings and ſixpence of Lord Dynevor to return one Hundred Guineas the firſt time he goes to a Maſquerade. 1807.

Mʳ. J. Talbot bets Genl. Bligh 2 guineas that Sir Arthur Welleſley is Gazetted for an Engliſh Peerage before this day three months. May 19ᵗʰ. 1809.

φευ, φευ, *occidit, occidit.*
Lord Frederick Bentinck bets Mʳ. Pybus 50 guineas that the eldeſt ſon of the late Earl of Berkeley now M.P. for Glouceſter-ſhire ſucceeds to the Earldom of Berkeley. Aug 10. 1810. *Spes omnis.*

Mʳ. Talbot bets Lord Henry Moore ten guineas that a certain event in which he is to be a principal actor & by which he is to gain the ſum of thirty thouſand pounds does not take place within two months from this time. March 8. 1811.

M^r. Conyers bets Ld de Clifford 15 guineas that the Irish Bank Tokens of 5 & 10 pence are of the standard value of the Spanish Dollar.　June 27.　1811.

Lord Conyngham bets Sir J. Copley three guineas that M^r. Tyrwhitt is now a Knight. 5 o'cl: May 7th.　1812.

M^r. Brummell bets M^r. Irby 100 g^s. to 10. that Buonaparte returns to Paris.　Dec. 12. 1812.

Sir James Craufurd bets M^r. Warrender ten guineas to one that if Bonaparte is dethroned he dies within a week.　1814.

M^r. Berkeley Paget bets Col. Stanhope five guineas that Sir George Talbot is confined in the Temple before Lord Castlereagh.　1814.

M^r. Drummond Burrell bets M^r. Berkeley Paget ten guineas that Napoleon or his

allies enter Vienna as Conquerors, and ten
guineas that he enters Berlin, againſt Eng-
land or its allies entering Paris. 21ˢᵗ April.
1814.

Sir George Talbot bets Lord Tyrconnell
five guineas that if the preſent Emperor of
the French ſhould offer to abide by that
part of the Peace of Paris that relates to
Boundaries as agreed to by Louis XVIII.
this country will not go to war with France.
March 24ᵗʰ. 1815.

Mʳ. Butler bets Sir George Talbot twenty
gˢ. to one that He is not in the Room at
White's with Napoleon, in the courſe of
the next two years. April 24. 1815.

Mʳ. Raikes bets Sir Joſ. Copley twenty-
five gˢ. that the French will be maſters of
Antwerp & Luxembourg againſt the Allies
being maſters of Paris in ſix months from
this day. 23 May. 1815.

Lord Yarmouth bets Col. Cooke one Hundred Guineas, that in the event of Bonaparte's death, the Duke of Orleans will be Sovereign of France, againſt any of the Napoleon family.   June 20th.   1815.

The Marqueſs of Conyngham bets Lord Alvanley 10 g^s. that Louis 18th. sits on the throne of France this day year.   June 19th. 1816.

M^r. Brodrick bets fifty guineas with Genl. Mackenzie on Sir John Shelley winning the Derby againſt Lord Stewart being married to Lady F. V. Tempeſt in ſix months from this day.   May 22^d.   1818.

Sir. G. Warrender bets Lord Alvanley one guinea that Lord Rancliffe being a member of the H. of Commons has no right to vote at the next election for a temporal Peer of Scotland.   1819.

L^d. Yarmouth gives L^d. Glengall five guineas to receive one hundred guineas if M^r. G. Brummell returns to London before Buonaparte returns to Paris. April, 1819.

M^r. Seymour Bathurſt takes Lord Foley's two guineas to one that Sir Robert Wilſon is either Commander in chief or hung this day ſix weeks. 1820.

Duke of Richmond bets Lord Caſſilis 10 to 1 that Napoleon has not eſcaped from S^t. Helena (in the Juno french frigate) as reported in the Courier of this day. Nov. 1. 1820.

www.ingramcontent.com/pod-product-compliance
Lightning Source LLC
Chambersburg PA
CBHW022021080426
42733CB00007B/670